F·R·E·S·H PRINCE OF Bel-Air

By
Lee Kilduff

kidsbooks®
Incorporated

Photo credits:

Cover: Globe Photos

Page   6: NBC
Page 10: Michael Benabib
Page 14: Janet Macoska
Page 18: NBC
Page 20: NBC
Page 24: NBC/Chris Haston
Page 26: Bob V. Noble/Globe Photos
Page 28: NBC/Globe Photos
Page 30: NBC
Page 36: Janet Macoska
Page 40: NBC
Page 42: NBC/Globe Photos
Page 46: Globe Photos
Page 48: NBC
Page 52: NBC
Page 58: NBC
Page 62: NBC/Globe Photos

Copyright © 1993 Kidsbooks, Inc.
7004 N. California Avenue
Chicago, IL 60645

ISBN: 1-56156-193-2

Manufactured in the United States of America

TABLE OF CONTENTS

Page

Introduction 5

Chapter 1: Will's Early Days 7

Chapter 2: The Fresh Prince and DJ Jazzy
             Jeff 13

Chapter 3: The Fresh Prince Hits Hollywood 17

Chapter 4: The Fresh Prince of Bel-Air 23

Chapter 5: Meet the Cast 27

Chapter 6: The Guys Keep Rapping 35

Chapter 7: Will on the Silver Screen 39

Chapter 8: Life with Will 43

Chapter 9: Fresh Facts 47

Chapter 10: Fresh Prince Trivia 49

Chapter 11: Last Words from Will 61

Chapter 1

Will's Early Days

Just like the character he plays on *The Fresh Prince of Bel-Air*, Will Smith grew up on the streets around Philadelphia.

Will was born into a middle-class family in Philadelphia on Sept. 25, 1970. The oldest son, Will was named for his father, Will Smith, Sr. The elder Smith kept a tight rein on his son. While his mother and father deeply loved Will, his brother, and two sisters, Will was always a little in awe of his father.

"My father had me under total control," Will recalls. "It's very important for a boy to grow up having such a strong male figure around. I always felt loved, but I was also scared of my dad."

Will grew up surrounded by a tight-knit family and by music. There were always a piano and drums around. Will loved to jam with his younger brother, Harry, and two sisters, Ellen and Pam. Six years older than Will, Pam was a big musical influence on her little brother.

"I was into making music with my family," Will remembers. "But I liked writing music better than playing." It's no accident that Will became the rapper—not the D.J.!

Will attended Overbrook High School in Winfield, PA where like any other teenager, he occasionally got into a little bit of trouble. But Will could talk his way out of almost anything—and looked good doing it. His teachers dubbed him: "Prince Charming." Will would later think of that nickname when he needed a tag to rap, pairing it with "fresh"—the new slang for cool.

Will's early years weren't all fun, though. When he was 13, his parents decided to divorce. While this was difficult for Will and his brother and sisters, he realized that his parents were better off apart.

"It brought peace to the house and to each parent," Will says. Will stayed close to both his parents. His father continued to be a strong influence on his growing son's life and he helped Will combat peer pressure.

"There was no peer pressure that could ever make me do anything I didn't want to," Will says. From his father, Will learned he could overcome almost any obstacle through hard work.

Once, when Will was 15 and his brother Harry was 12, their father made them fix a crumbling wall in front of his business. To repair the wall, Will and Harry had to tear it down and rebuild it.

"I kept thinking 'this is impossible, this is totally impossible,'" Will recalls. "I knew I'd be building that wall for the rest of my life." Not quite. But the wall did take the brothers more than six months to complete.

It wasn't until years later that Will learned why his father had asked him to tackle the job of rebuilding the wall. Will's father wanted his sons to learn that they could accomplish something that at first seemed impossible.

"There are always going to be walls in life," Will says. "He helped us get over one, so that we'd never be scared to take the first step and try to do the impossible." It was a lesson Will never forgot.

As Will grew up, there was another big influence in his life: music.

At an early age Will tried writing poems and short stories. But something was missing. When he heard the Sugarhill Gang's "Rapper's Delight," Will knew he wanted to try rapping himself.

By the time he was 12 Will was seeking out parties where he could try his hand at rapping. At that point, Will wasn't too different from many other Philadelphia area youths. It seemed like almost everyone wanted to take a whack at rapping. Will was no exception.

"Everybody has a rap," Will says. "Let's say your friend was to have a party. I have a rap, and there's a D.J., so I'll say my rap. It was just a hobby."

**DJ Jazzy Jeff and The Fresh Prince
turn rap into fun.**

Will wasn't yet thinking about a musical career. He was thinking about expressing himself. As time passed he began to find his own voice. He also learned he could use rap to make people laugh.

Will paid more and more attention to the hip-hop sound. He listened to cassettes from New York record parties showcasing Treacherous 3, the Sugar Hill Gang, and Kurtis Blow—the founding fathers of "Rap Nation."

In the same town, a guy named Jeff Townes was getting his own reputation—but it was as a master of the turntable. Jeff could spin and mix and cut with the best of the disc jockeys. Rap was his sound!

"When rap came out, there was this buzz: This was something new," recalls Jeff. "We never heard this before but somebody made this just for us. This is our music because our parents don't like it, our grandmothers don't like it, but we like it."

Will and Jeff had heard of each other but they had never met. Then, one day in 1986, Will and Jeff both turned up at a house party on Will's mother's block. It turned out to be an important night for both guys.

Something special was born when Will grabbed the mike.

"He started rapping and I started cutting and it was like natural chemistry," Jeff says. "He flowed with what I did and I flowed exactly with what he did and we knew it. We just clicked the whole night long. We were laughing and joking like we'd known each other for 10 years."

Will and Jeff both went home from the party that night knowing they would soon get to know each other better. They had to. Together, Will and Jeff could swing any party in Philadelphia—and it didn't have to stop there!

Chapter 2

The Fresh Prince and DJ Jazzy Jeff

Soon after Will and Jeff paired up the prince faced a major decision. Then 17, Will had been offered a scholarship to the Massachusetts Institute of Technology. Should he take it or try to make it big with Jazzy Jeff?

It's not hard to figure out what happened next. Will said "no thanks" to MIT and started riding toward success in the music business.

"My parents figured I'd do (rap) for a couple of minutes and then go to college," Will recalls. "But things started to take off."

And they started to take off fast. In the summer of 1986, DJ Jazzy Jeff and The Fresh Prince released their first single, "Girls Ain't Nothing But Trouble." The single was as fresh as the prince. It became a top 10 hit in England and brought the

**DJ Jazzy Jeff and The Fresh Prince
soar to the heights of musical success.**

duo to the attention of Jive Records in the United States.

In 1987, the pair released their first album: "Rock the House." The album featured both "Girls Ain't Nothing But Trouble" and the clever answer, "Boys Ain't Nothing But Trouble."

After releasing the album, the pair hit the road with the LL Cool J Def Jam tour.

But it was their second album that sent Will and Jeff exploding toward success. "He's the D.J., I'm the Rapper" sold 2.5 million copies and gave birth to two major hits: "Parents Just Don't Understand" and "Nightmare on My Street."

The album was snapped up by fans. It also helped make rap popular among teens who liked rap's beat but not some of the hard-edged lyrics they had heard from other rap stars. It was a great time for Will and Jeff. The two even started a 900 number that fans could call for information about them which was a whopping success.

In 1988, Will and Jeff won their first Grammy —the highest honor in the music business. Their fans sure understood why! Other honors followed. Will and Jeff accepted two American Music Awards, an MTV Music Award, and a Soul Train Music Award nomination.

Will and Jeff were now on their way. The dynamic duo kept moving, going back on the road with Run-DMC, Public Enemy, EPMD, and Stetasonic.

"It was fun," Will says. "I thought, if these people are foolish enough to pay me for something I was going to do anyway, then O.K."

Almost from the beginning one thing set Will and Jeff apart from many of their fellow rappers— humor. Will was one funny guy and he and Jeff liked recording hits that cracked their fans up.

"Rap is a music based on being the best through arguing, insulting, and verbally battling with each other," Will says. "It's about competition. But I don't think it has to be angry. In fact, when it first started, rap was about having fun."

As Will and Jeff continued working together they learned more and more to rely on each other's strengths. Will is the wit. Jazzy Jeff is the music master.

"Will has always been the front man, he's the focal point," Jeff says. "Will is completely out there, he's crazy, he goes too far. Me, I'm too laid back. I just sit and chill all the time. When he gets too far out, I pull him back. When I'm too laid back, he pulls me out." Together, they make a cool sound.

DJ Jazzy Jeff and The Fresh Prince's third album was called "And, I'm In This Corner." That album's biggest hit, "I Think I Can Beat Mike Tyson," was just as funny as anything they had done before.

By then, however, Will was ready to make people laugh in another way, and Hollywood was ready to give him that chance!

Chapter 3

The Fresh Prince Hits Hollywood

Will attracted attention from television network officials after performing a rap version of a song from *Mary Poppins* as part of Disneyland's 35th Anniversary Celebration. Will seemed likable, charming, and had presence. The network people were impressed with what they saw.

Meanwhile, while appearing on the *Arsenio Hall Show,* Will met Benny Medina, then a vice-president at Warner Bros. Records. Will and Medina instantly hit it off, talking about basketball and other interests they shared.

The next day, Medina told Will he wanted to do a show that would be loosely based on his own life. Medina, whose mother had died when he was young, was raised around Los Angeles in foster homes. Eventually Medina met a white composer

**Will Smith—tall and lean—
the hottest thing to hit the TV scene!**

for films who became fond of him. He invited Medina to live with him and his family in their Beverly Hills home. Soon, Medina was the only black student at Beverly Hills High School. However, because the idea seemed similar to another show, *Diff'rent Strokes*, that was already on the air, Medina made a big change.

The street-smart kid who Will would play would go to live with rich black people.

"When I told him the idea," Medina recalls, "he was thrilled." Medina put Will in touch with Quincy Jones who would be producing the show.

Although he had no acting experience, Will was soon asked to audition for Jones and top NBC executives. Although he was on tour at the time he traveled 17 hours to get to the audition.

"It happened pretty quickly," Will remembers. But, at the time, he also knew he was ready to try acting. To Will the part seemed made to order.

"When this came up, I said to myself, 'this is my shot,'" Will recalls. "I'm taking whatever happens. This was my thing and I was going to do it." Will also knew that no matter what happened he would always have his music.

As it turned out, Will was a natural. Jones told Will that his comic talents more than made up for his lack of acting experience.

"You're walking the right way," Jones told Will. "So, until you bump into something, we're not going to stop you."

Jones, a music legend who has collected 19 Grammys of his own, remembers thinking that

The cast of *The Fresh Prince of Bel-Air*.

Will was a natural. He thinks Will's background as a rapper had a lot to do with that.

"He has high self esteem," Jones says of Will. "I guess you have to if you're going to be a rapper. People pay $15 to go to a house party and if you're no good, the crowd lets you know pretty quickly. Those are the kinds of parties where Will started." Jones says rap can be similar to slapstick comedy at times.

"I think that's why he's such a natural on television," Jones says.

The Fresh Prince of Bel-Air went on the air in the fall of 1990. Almost immediately, it was being hailed as a sure hit for NBC.

Will, who uses his own name on the show, stars as a tough inner-city youth who is sent off to live with his rich aunt and uncle after getting into trouble in his native west Philadelphia neighborhood. Will says his character is something of an updated version of the Beverly Hillbillies. That once-popular show, which can still be seen in reruns, featured a poor mountain family who discovered oil on their land. After striking it rich, the Clampetts moved to Beverly Hills, CA.

Much like the Clampetts, Will must adjust to a very different life than the one he had lived back home. The culture shock that Will experiences makes for some hilarious episodes.

The prince must deal with his Uncle Philip, a successful attorney who doesn't always understand him. His Aunt Vivian tries to keep harmony in the family, which includes Will's three cousins.

There's the beautiful Hillary, a spoiled brat, and the ultra-preppie Carlton, who likes to point out Will's faults. The youngest child, Ashley, is usually in Will's corner. Perhaps the snootiest member of the household is the family butler, Geoffrey.

Will and his adoptive family sometimes clash. But, during the three seasons the show has been on the air they have also gained some understanding of each other. Will may argue with his uncle, but if outsiders criticize Uncle Philip, look out!

The prince likes the fact that his show features different types of black people.

"Everyone is represented on the show," Will says. "My aunt represents the middle. Her husband is snooty."

The show has fans of all ages, races, and economic groups. It's hard not to like the prince!

Chapter 4

The Fresh Prince of Bel-Air

In some ways, Will is a lot like the good-natured character he plays. But in other ways the two couldn't be more different. The real-life Will is an incredibly hard worker who admits to being a perfectionist when it comes to his show.

Will tries to make his show as hilarious as it can be.

"If the show isn't as funny as it should have been, I can't sleep," Will says. "We have to go back and redo it. I'm not crazy and if I don't think it's funny, other people won't think it's funny."

A lot of people have a hand in putting the show together. Will gives much of the credit for the show's success to the writers, producers, directors, and other creative people he works with.

"There are a lot of people who go into the

**The Fresh Prince poses with his on-screen cousins:
Hillary, Ashley, and Carlton.**

making of *Fresh Prince*," Will explains. "Without them, I'm just another funny guy."

But because Will is such a funny guy, he likes to ad-lib while he's rehearsing. The funniest lines that Will says are added by the writers to the scripts that are used when the show is taped.

Since going on the air, Will says he has learned a lot about how to say a line so it is as funny as it can be. Will may not have known a lot about acting when he started *Fresh Prince*, but he sure learned fast.

"I like the show because it's always fresh, I'm always learning," Will says. "My acting gets better with each episode. I mean I think it does."

One way Will has improved his acting is by paying attention to his audiences' reactions. The cast tapes *Fresh Prince* in front of a live audience —something Will loves doing.

"It gets your energy up to go out in front of a live audience," he says. Luckily for Will, he had a lot of experience performing live from the tours he had done as a rapper.

Although Will works hard, he says the *Fresh Prince* set is also "the most fun place" he has ever worked. And, according to Karyn Parsons, who plays Hillary, Will is a big reason for that.

"Will is great fun," she says, "but he gets me in trouble all the time."

**The cast of *The Fresh Prince of Bel-Air*
with guest stars.**

Chapter 5

Meet the Cast

Are you ready to meet the rest of the *Fresh Prince* cast?

The head of the Banks family is Uncle Philip, played by James Avery. Avery was born and raised in Atlantic City, N.J., where he attended high school. After graduation, Avery joined the U.S. Navy. From 1968 to 1969, he served in Vietnam.

Following his discharge from the Navy, Avery settled in San Diego, CA. He began writing poetry and television scripts for the Public Broadcasting Station. Eventually he won an Emmy Award, the highest honor in television, for a show called *Almeda Speaks and the Poet*. Avery won a scholarship to the University of California at San Diego and earned a Bachelor of Arts degree in Drama and Literature.

**The Fresh Prince gets one over
on his aunt and uncle.**

After working at the Oregon Shakespeare Festival in Ashland, Oregon, Avery moved to Los Angeles to try his luck with television. Before joining the *Fresh Prince* cast, Avery appeared in many commercials and television shows, including *St. Elsewhere, Beauty and the Beast,* and *Simple Justice.* He continues to play a recurring role on *L.A. Law.* Avery's film credits include *Fletch, License to Drive,* and *Eight Million Ways to Die.*

When he's not acting Avery says he likes "anything to do with water." You might find him sailing, swimming, snorkeling, or scuba-diving.

Avery and his wife have two foster children.

Luckily for Will, Avery's character is married to Aunt Vivian, who is played by Janet Hubert-Whitten. After attending high school in her native Momence, IL Hubert-Whitten won a scholarship to the world-famous Julliard School in Manhattan, where she concentrated on theater.

Hubert-Whitten first appeared professionally as part of the national touring company of the Broadway hit *Dancin'.* She later made it to Broadway, appearing in the original cast of *Cats.* She also appeared in Broadway productions of *Joseph and the Amazing Technicolor Dreamcoat* and *The First,* and in an Off-Broadway production of *Anteroom.*

In Monte Carlo, Hubert-Whitten performed a one-woman show at the Sporting Club.

Hubert-Whitten is also no stranger to television. She appeared regularly in the daytime soap opera, *One Life to Live.* She has also guest-starred

**Karyn Parsons plays Hillary Banks.
She is smart and beautiful.**

on such shows as *21 Jump Street*, *Hunter*, *Hooperman*, and *All My Children*.

This versatile actress has also appeared on the big screen in *A Piece of the Action* and *Agent on Ice*.

Hubert-Whitten lives in Los Angeles. Her hobbies include horseback riding and playing tennis. She also enjoys strumming on her guitar.

The oldest Banks child is the stuck-up Hillary, played by Karyn Parsons.

Karyn was born and raised in Los Angeles, where she began studying acting at age 13. After graduating from Santa Monica High School in California, Karyn set out to follow her dream of becoming an actress. But it didn't happen overnight.

Karyn was working as a hostess in a restaurant when she learned she had won the part of Hillary.

"I flipped," she remembers. "I went out of my mind. Everyone kept telling me, 'Go home, go celebrate.'" Instead, Karyn kept the job until she was sure the *Fresh Prince* show would make it.

The sweet, likable Karyn is nothing like the pampered rich girl she plays. About the only thing Karyn likes about Hillary is her clothes! But Karyn says Hillary is tons of fun to play.

Karyn calls Hillary a "Daddy's girl" who is very spoiled and self-centered.

"She was the first child and a girl, so her parents indulged her and babied her," says Karyn of Hillary. "I don't think they realized what the outcome would be."

Karyn's days at Santa Monica High gave her a few ideas about how Hillary should be played. She said she "borrowed" some of Hillary's phrases and characteristics from different girls she knew in high school.

Karyn has appeared in many commercials. She has also guest-starred on the series *Hunter*. In 1992, she hit the big screen in the comedy *Class Act*.

In her spare time—which she doesn't have too much of these days—Karyn loves to dance, horseback-ride, fence, and scuba dive. She also enjoys photography and making porcelain dolls.

Karyn also finds time to be active in the organization Love Is Feeding Everyone or LIFE.

Hillary's preppie brother Carlton is played by Alfonso Ribeiro. The New York City native broke into acting early. He began his professional career at age eight, when he appeared on the PBS drama series *Ole Willie*. Television viewers later saw Alfonso when he starred on the NBC series *Silver Spoons*.

Alfonso's other television credits include *Magnum P.I.*, *Circus of the Stars*, *The Andy Williams Christmas Special*, and *Star Cruise*. Alfonso is also at home on the stage. He created the leading role of Willie in the original cast of the 1984 Broadway musical *Tap Dance Kid*. If you think his voice sounds familiar you might have heard it on several single recordings, including "Dance Baby," "Not Too Young (To Fall in Love)," "Time Bomb," and "Sneak Away with Me."

When he's not playing sports, Alfonso likes racing cars and riding motorcycles. He lives in Los Angeles with his parents and two older brothers.

The youngest Banks daughter, Ashley, is played by Tatyana M. Ali who, at 13, is already a television veteran.

Young viewers may know Tatyana from her days on *Sesame Street*, where she appeared from 1984 to 1988. Other viewers may have seen her guest appearances on *The Cosby Show* or the daytime soap *All My Children.*

A two-time winner in the singing competition on *Star Search*, Tatyana has starred in the *Sports Illustrated For Kids Olympic Special.* On Broadway, she appeared with James Earl Jones as part of the original cast of *Fences.* She played Off-Broadway roles in productions of *Sugar Hill* and *Orfeo del Campo.*

Tatyana's film credits include Eddie Murphy's *Raw* and *Crocodile Dundee II.*

The Long Island, N.Y. native enjoys singing, dancing, gymnastics, and swimming. She lives with her parents and two younger sisters, Anastasia and Kimberly.

The Banks family could never survive without their butler Geoffrey, brought to life by Joseph Marcell.

Marcell made his American series debut on *The Fresh Prince of Bel-Air.* But the British-bred Marcell has been in the acting business for the past 20 years.

Born on the Caribbean island of St. Lucia, Marcell was five when he and his family moved to England.

Marcell had planned to be an engineer. He changed his mind after watching a performance by the Negro Ensemble Theater in London. Marcell studied at Sheffield University in Yorkshire, graduating from the Central School of Speech and Dance.

As a member of the prestigious Royal Shakespeare Company, Marcell appeared in productions of *A Midsummer Night's Dream, Antony and Cleopatra,* and *Macbeth.* He acted in many other stage plays in London, including *Joe Turner's Come and Gone, Black Star, Sherlock Holmes,* and *One Fine Day.*

Marcell starred in the British television series' *Empire Road, Juliet Bravo,* and *Fancy Wanders.* Among his film credits are *Cry Freedom* and *Playing Away.*

Because of his continuing love for the stage, Marcell serves on the board of the Old Globe Theater and the Temba Theater Company.

Chapter 6

The Guys Keeps Rapping

Many rap fans feared that the Fresh Prince would stop rapping when his television show proved so popular. They figured DJ Jazzy Jeff would move onto something new.

But the Fresh Prince and DJ Jazzy Jeff liked making music together and they planned to keep right on doing it!

So, while Will took on Hollywood, Jazzy Jeff stayed in the studio working on the duo's sound. Of course, once in a while, he traveled to Hollywood to appear on his buddy's show. But mostly Jeff concentrated on recreating the group's sound. Once he had the beat, Will worked on the words.

In 1991, the pair's fans got what they'd been waiting for: another great album. The duo's fourth album, called "Homebase," became a platinum-

Will and Jeff do the talk show scene.

seller, producing the hits "Summertime" and "Ring My Bell." With "Summertime," the pair won their second Grammy for the Best Performance by a Duo or Group.

The album was almost completely different from anything they had done before. The only thing that stayed the same was the humor that runs through all of their work.

"Music changes," Jazzy Jeff says. "I changed, I grew, the music had to change."

And, change it did! Will and Jeff describe "Homebase" as a record you can listen and dance to.

"You want to dance," Jeff says, "but you can sit back and listen to every song on the album." One reason that the album had a different sound to it was that Jeff expanded the cutting and scratching sound of rap by adding live instruments, real drumming, and live back-up singers. Will loves the new sound.

"It's the way to go these days," says the prince. "It added to the studio experience in that so many other elements came into play and helped the creative process in a lot of different ways."

"Homebase" opens with "I'm All That," a sly dissing of the group's critics.

Cutting a slice from Kool & The Gang's "Summer Madness" DJ Jazzy Jeff and The Fresh Prince fashioned the hit "Summertime," a shimmering heat wave of good times and block parties, hoses and hot dogs. Will says he hopes "Summertime" was the kind of hit that would forever remind fans of the summer of 1991.

"Every year, there's that one record that stands out in everyone's mind," he says.

On the album, the Fresh Prince rapped through a series of different voices. He's a private eye on "Who Stole the D.J.?"; a cool Casanova on "This Boy is Smooth"; and a dreamer on "Trapped On the Dance Floor."

Don't expect "Homebase" to be the last time you hear from the popular kings of hip-hop. Will and Jazzy Jeff have been working on a new album. This time, however, they're doing the work on different coasts!

Jeff records all the music from his home base in Philadelphia, then he sends it out to Will. Will goes to a West Coast studio and adds the lyrics.

"We know each other well enough to work like this," Will says.

And, with all of Will's activities, it's the only way he has time to keep rapping.

Chapter 7

Will On the Silver Screen

Almost as soon as Will started acting on television, he began dreaming of making a movie. To him, it seemed like a natural next step. It seemed like the next step to the movie industry as well!

But Will didn't want to be in just any movie. He wanted to be sure he landed the right role. Will and Jazzy Jeff turned down the first film they were offered. Their roles in that movie, *House Party*, were eventually played by Kid 'n Play.

In 1990, even before NBC knew for sure that the *Fresh Prince* show would be a hit, 20th Century Fox signed Will to a two-movie deal.

At first, it seemed as if Will would star in a "buddy film" that would feature him as a policeman. But Will then decided to put movie projects on hold while he worked on making the *Fresh Prince*

Check it out! Will Smith wants you!

show the smash it now is.

Will's first dip into the movie world came in 1991, when he accepted a small role in an independent movie called *Where the Day Takes You*. Released in September, 1992, the film features Will as a homeless teen in a wheelchair. Will took the part because it gave him a chance to try a serious role.

"He's in a wheelchair, living on the streets— pretty much a bum," says Will of the character he played.

The movie, which costarred Sean Astin, Dermot Mulroney, Balthazar Getty, Lara Flynn, and other young celebs, also attracted Will's interest because of the issues it tackled.

In the movie, Mulroney's character heads up a group of homeless teens trying to live on the streets of Los Angeles. Will's character and the other members of the crew survive by using various hustles. Much of the movie unfolds as Mulroney's character is interviewed by a social worker, played by Laura San Giacomo.

Making the film was an eye opener for Will!

"I was in full makeup on Hollywood Boulevard and people didn't know me," he recalls. "Just seeing how people ignore the homeless was an amazing lesson. It was a revelation seeing how cold people can be."

Will's next movie will be entirely different. He will appear in *Change of Heart*, starring Ted Danson—the lovable Sam on the long-running comedy *Cheers*—and the queen of comedy, Whoopi Goldberg.

Will Smith is one happening guy!

Chapter 8

Life With Will

By now you must be wondering how Will does it all—rap, television, and movies. How does this guy fit everything in? And where does he get his strength?

For one thing, Will doesn't mind 15-hour work days.

"I guess I get my strength from working," he says. "As long as I get my eight hours of sleep, I'm fine."

Will has to be on the *Fresh Prince* set by nine a.m. He usually stays until after five p.m. When the prince and DJ Jazzy Jeff are recording, Will leaves the television set and heads right for the recording studio. Sometimes he'll work until midnight!

One way Will keeps his life together is by keeping his two loves largely separate. Some of the older fans of the *Fresh Prince* show don't even know Will is a hit rapper.

"What we tried to do was make sure the TV show was totally separate from Jazzy Jeff and the Fresh Prince," Jeff says. "I think we did a really good job."

Will has also brought peace to his personal life. He has learned to handle success—and the money and fame that came with it.

That wasn't always true. When Will first made it as a rapper he'd go on wild spending sprees. He would buy games, pool tables, and anything else that caught his eye.

"I wasn't trying to manage my money, I was trying to spend it," he recalls. "I was 18 with a Grammy award and millions of dollars at my fingertips. I spent it all. Then I started getting myself together." Will is now much more concerned about planning for the future. And, a woman named Sheree Zampino Smith has a lot to do with that!

Will married Sheree in the spring of 1992. First, they had a double-ring ceremony. Following the ceremony, the couple and 125 of their closest friends and family enjoyed a lavish reception at a hotel in Santa Barbara, CA. Among those helping them celebrate were DJ Jazzy Jeff and actor Denzel Washington.

Will was never one to date many women, and was happy to settle down. "The time you would spend chasing women around is valuable time and you need to use that time enlightening yourself or making yourself stronger for the business world,"

Will explains. "You just waste a lot of time at the clubs on Fridays trying to find a girl, and in the malls, and church. You waste time and energy, time and energy better spent working on your future."

But more importantly, Will is madly in love with Sheree. He tries to spend as much time as possible with her. If the day is a busy one, the two might meet for lunch on the set. Will and Sheree try to live as much of a "non-Hollywood life" as possible, avoiding many of the parties that are constantly going on in the glitzy town.

Recently, Will and Sheree found another reason to stay home. They now have their very own prince to play with! Sheree gave birth to the couple's first child, a boy, in November.

Ironically, Sheree went into labor on a day Will was supposed to be rehearsing for a show in which the prince helps deliver a baby.

"When Will didn't show up for rehearsals, we all went 'Uh, Oh,'" remembers actress Vanessa Williams, who played the new mom on the episode. Sure enough, Will was at the hospital with Sheree being a real-life labor coach.

Will's personal life is now just as wonderful as his professional life!

Musician Will Smith grooves to his tunes.

Chapter 9

Fresh Facts

Name: Will Smith
Birthdate: Sept. 25, 1970
Birthplace: Philadelphia, PA.
Height: 6 feet, 3 inches
Hair color: Brown
Eye color: Brown
Wife: Sheree Zampino Smith
Favorite comedian: Eddie Murphy. Will thinks his own antics are pretty funny too!
Nickname: His teachers called him "Prince" because he was so charming. He teamed Prince with Fresh, which in 1985 was the newest street slang for "cool."
Favorite hobbies: Basketball, pool, and hanging out with Sheree.
Address: Write to Will Smith, c/o *The Fresh Prince of Bel-Air*, NBC Television, 3000 West Alameda Blvd., Burbank, CA 91523

**Offscreen, Will hangs with co-stars
Karyn Parsons and Alfonso Ribeiro.**

Chapter 10

Fresh Prince Trivia

Do you think you know all there is to know about Will Smith, *The Fresh Prince of Bel-Air*, and Will's rap career? Well, get ready to find out just how much you really do know!

First try this fun quiz on the *Fresh Prince* show. Don't worry, you won't be graded!

Circle the correct choice:

1. **Will is sent to Bel-Air because he:**
   a. Gets into a fight
   b. Does poorly in school
   c. Plays too much basketball
2. **On the show, Hillary lives in:**
   a. The main house
   b. The pool house
   c. A nearby apartment building

3. **Uncle Philip became a _____ af-ter the victorious candidate died following an argument with Will.**
   a. Congressman
   b. Judge
   c. District attorney

4. **Will's biggest ally in the Banks family is:**
   a. Carlton
   b. Hillary
   c. Ashley

5. **The Fresh Prince show is loosely based on the life of:**
   a. Benny Medina
   b. Will Smith
   c. Quincy Jones

6. **The term that best describes Carlton is:**
   a. Fun
   b. Friendly
   c. Preppie

7. **Will moves to Bel-Air from:**
   a. New York City
   b. Philadelphia
   c. Los Angeles

8. **Will's mother is related to:**
   a. Aunt Vivian
   b. Uncle Philip
   c. None of the above

9. **One of Will's favorite activities is:**
   a. Doing homework
   b. Dating young women
   c. Hanging out with Carlton

Ready for more? Try your hand at this true/false test about the whole *Fresh Prince* gang.

1. James Avery, who plays Uncle Philip, has a recurring role on *L.A. Law.* __T__F
2. Karyn Parsons, who plays Hillary, was working as a saleswoman when she found out she'd landed a spot on *Fresh Prince.* __T__F
3. Will Smith has one sister. __T__F
4. Karyn Parsons was born and bred in Los Angeles, CA. __T__F
5. Tatyana Ali, who plays Ashley, was a regular on *Mr. Roger's Neighborhood.* __T__F
6. Karyn Parsons had a regular role on the show *A Different World* before joining *Fresh Prince.* __T__F
7. Joseph Marcell, otherwise known as Geoffrey, grew up in England. __T__F
8. Before he became Carlton, Alfonso Ribeiro acted on the NBC series *Silver Spoons.* __T__F
9. Will Smith stopped rapping after the *Fresh Prince* show hit the air. __T__F
10. Janet Hubert-Whitten appeared in the original cast of the Broadway hit *Cats.* __T__F

Here's a crossword puzzle on Will Smith and the *Fresh Prince* gang.

Across

1. Will and Jazzy Jeff scored a huge hit with an album whose title described both of them. What word described Will?
2. Jazzy Jeff's last name is _____.
3. Will put an end to his days as a _____ when he married Sheree.
4. Word that describes Will.
5. The oldest Banks child is _____.

Down

1. Their fourth album, _____, produced the hit "Summertime."
2. Will's teachers used to call him _____.
3. Will first travels through Bel-Air in a _____.
4. One of Will's favorite hobbies is playing _____.

The Fresh Prince of Bel-Air

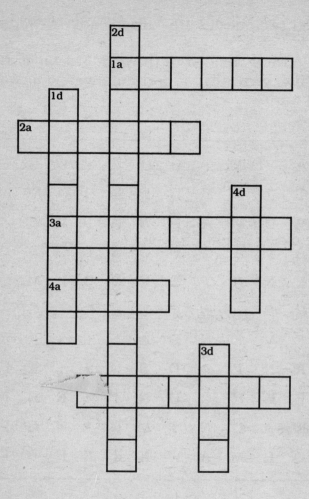

The next two puzzles are called Search-A-Words.

Find the words hidden in the grid. They may run diagonally, vertically, or horizontally, and forward or backward.

A	A	V	W	T	B	O	P	Y	Z	L	Z
V	T	R	O	U	B	L	E	S	O	M	E
B	M	U	M	A	U	B	H	I	V	Y	Z
W	A	V	A	G	F	O	S	I	O	S	B
O	R	K	N	T	E	V	D	Q	F	M	G
K	E	S	I	W	T	E	E	R	T	S	E
K	F	V	Z	N	D	A	E	A	X	R	R
L	R	N	E	A	D	S	N	J	I	K	L
I	E	W	R	C	H	N	I	Z	R	E	F
L	W	A	G	N	I	M	R	A	H	C	R
A	O	B	M	A	W	X	I	X	H	B	E

Find these words that describe Will's character:

Kind   Streetwise   Womanizer

Charming   Troublesome   Fresh

```
M  A  V  H  E  I  X  I  S  M  N  S
A  L  L  B  S  B  A  X  P  I  P  O
R  B  R  O  L  I  L  M  O  O  O  I
V  L  I  I  V  V  F  M  I  L  B  P
E  E  E  I  G  E  O  L  L  A  M  N
L  T  V  B  I  S  W  X  E  D  E  V
O  I  E  V  A  Y  B  D  S  O  L
B  R  A  T  T  Y  Q  D  C  I  P  M
E  T  I  I  V  D  E  L  D  A  O  I
R  Y  A  D  E  R  E  P  M  A  P  N
V  T  L  M  P  O  I  L  M  B  D  O
A  B  R  A  S  B  A  E  L  I  O  V
```

Search out these words that describe Hillary:

Spoiled   Daddy's girl   Selfish

Pampered   Bratty   Trite

**Handsome Alfonso Ribeiro
plays preppie Carlton Banks.**

Answer Key:

Multiple choice: 1/a, 2/b, 3/b, 4/c, 5/a, 6/c, 7/b, 8/a, 9/b, 10/b

Fill in the Blanks: 1/ Grammy, 2/ England, 3/ Overbrook, 4/ Rock the House, 5/ block party, 6/ And In This Corner, 7/ *Where the Day Takes You,* 8/ Pam, 9/ *Mary Poppins,* 10/ Eddie Murphy

True/False: 1/ true, 2/ false, 3/ false, 4/ true, 5/ false, 6/ false, 7/true, 8/ true, 9/ false 10/ true

The Fresh Prince of Bel-Air

Crossword Puzzle

```
              P
           R  A  P  P  E  R
        H  I
  T  O  W  N  E  S
        M  C
        E  E           P
        B  A  C  H  E  L  O  R
        A  H           O
        S  T  A  R     L
        E  H
           A
           R
           M        T
     H  I  L  L  A  R  Y
           N        X
           G        I
```

SAW #1

```
A  A  V  W  T  B  O  P  Y  Z  L  Z
V  T  R  O  U  B  L  E  S  O  M  E
B  M  U  M  A  U  B  H  I  V  Y  Z
W  A  V  A  G  F  O  S  I  O  S  B
O  R  K  N  T  E  V  D  O  F  M  G
K  E  S  I  W  T  E  E  R  T  S  E
K  F  V  Z  N  D  A  E  A  X  R  R
L  R  N  E  A  D  S  N  J  I  K  L
I  E  W  R  C  H  N  I  Z  R  E  F
L  W  A  G  N  I  M  R  A  H  C  R
A  O  B  M  A  W  X  I  X  H  B  E
```

SAW #2

```
M  A  V  H  E  I  X  I  S  M  N  S
A  L  B  S  B  A  X  P  I  P  O
R  B  R  O  L  I  L  M  O  O  O  I
V  L  I  V  V  F  M  I  L  B  P
E  E  E  I  G  E  O  L  L  A  M  N
L  T  V  B  I  S  W  X  E  D  E  V
O  I  E  V  A  V  Y  B  D  S  O  L
B  R  A  T  T  Y  G  D  C  I  P  M
E  T  I  I  V  D  E  L  D  A  O  I
R  Y  A  D  E  R  E  P  M  A  P  N
V  T  L  M  P  O  I  L  M  B  D  O
A  B  R  A  S  B  A  E  L  I  O  V
```

Chapter 11

Last Words from Will

Will on the differences between himself and the character he plays:
"I have a lot of business savvy and I am less of a playboy. Although we share the same sense of humor and attitude, there are a lot of things that get by him that wouldn't get by me."

Will on the way he's lived his life:
"I've always had my eye on the ball. I never slipped too much. Whenever I had a dream, I always had a plan. And, I have a lot of people in my corner trying to point me in the right direction."

**Don't you think The Fresh Prince fits right in
with his Beverly Hills cousins? Not!**

Will on the difference between being funny as a rapper and as an actor:

"Being able to be funny on wax isn't the same as being funny on camera. Because on wax it's all done in the studio, alone. You do it, you finish it, it's over. In TV, what's actually written on the paper isn't what makes you funny. It's how you say what's on the paper, it's how you stand, and it's how you respond—all those things. It's easy to be funny on a record . . . if you have funny lyrics."

Will on his favorite episode:

"My favorite episode was the mistaken identity episode, when Carlton and I get thrown in jail because the cops thought we stole this fancy car. But we were really just driving it for a rich friend of my uncle's. That's my favorite kind of show. It was hilariously funny and it had a message. That's what I like to get across in my show."

Will speaking about his faith in himself:

"I don't get nervous. I look at my neighborhood—I know personally 15 people who could be doing what I'm doing right now. But they're scared to take that shot. If they give me the position, I'll shoot my shot. The only thing that can go wrong is, I miss. And if I miss I'll shoot again."

Will on being a celebrity:

"I always thought I'd do something, but this is beyond my dreams. When I look back and see what it could have been like—all the things that might have gone wrong, all the pitfalls I avoided, it's like, if I had slept another 30 seconds or took another five seconds to tie my shoe, I wouldn't have been in the right place."